Reflections
A JOURNEY WITHIN

DANIEL C. HAYNES

ISBN:
979-8-9899598-8-4

DEDICATION

To you, my fellow traveler. I pray you find places where your presence blossoms in open spaces, and your gardens are continuously watered as you journey down life's winding road.

CONTENTS

ACKNOWLEDGMENTS

To the ones that stood like lighthouses when I've stumbled around
at my worst searching for myself, thank you.

For 215

INTRODUCTION

Dear Reader,

Welcome to this collection of letters, a tribute to the journey that is life, composed not merely of words but rather emotions, experiences, and insights, gathered and woven together to form a tapestry of wisdom and understanding.

These letters, penned with careful thought and earnest heart, carry whispers of courage, echoes of self-love, and reverberations of purpose. They explore the familiar yet profound dimensions of life - the struggles and the victories, the joy and the pain, the fear, and the hope. Each letter unfolds like a petal, revealing a new aspect of the intricate flower that is human existence.

They serve as gentle reminders of the innate strength and resilience we all carry within us, even in moments when we feel we are at our weakest. They encourage us to extend to ourselves the same compassion we bestow upon others, to seek purpose in our experiences, and to find solace and rejuvenation in the world around us.

"Reflections: A Journey Within" is a voyage through life's hills and valleys, an exploration within the labyrinth of self, with each piece offering a different lens to view our existence. It invites you to pause and ponder, to question and understand, to seek and find. Above all, it is a call to embrace who you are and who you are becoming, with grace and courage.

Whether you're feeling lost amidst the chaos of the city or searching for answers on a quiet evening, these letters serve as companions, offering solace, encouragement, and a friendly nudge towards growth. Like a soft glow in the darkness, they aim to guide you towards finding peace, purpose, and fulfillment in your own journey.

As you delve into this collection, you will find that each section will conclude with a few blank pages inviting you, dear reader, to embark on your own inner journey and document your thoughts, reflections, or even your own creative expressions. See these blank pages as your canvas— a space for you to weave your own stories, explore your emotions, and perhaps find your own wisdom within the tapestry of this book. And when you reach the end of this book, you will also find a dedicated section with ample blank pages for your personal reflections, ensuring that your own journey of self-discovery continues long after you've turned the final page.

Embark on this journey, and may you find in these letters a mirror that reflects your joys and sorrows, your hopes and fears, your dreams, and realities. But most importantly, may you see in them a reflection of the love you truly deserve.

With all my heart,
Daniel C. Haynes

Reflections

REFLECTIVE & ENCOURAGING

You,

I write this letter to you on spring days,
where the sun shines his face brilliantly,
his rays like fingers
                    dancing across your skin,
leaving it glistening

And as you find renewal in the freshness of the breeze
carrying the smells of life across your nostrils
as you step into the world around you
you'll find it receptive to your every wish
as you shape the day to your molding.

I pray you'll find peace in the knowledge that
everything will be okay,
and that all things work together for good,
orchestrated in your favor by your faith.

You,

I write this letter to you so that on the days
where worlds collide
and you find yourself surrounded by familiarity,

Embraced warmly by ones you've long missed,
whose voices once sat on the other end of a phone,
now surround sound your present

You'll remember to take a minute,
to live in the moment
and breathe in its air

letting burdens, once carried alone
rise off your shoulders,
lifted now by collective strength.

I pray that you find that
feeling of comfort and peace
in every day
as you navigate
the waters
of life.

You,

I write this letter to you so that on spring nights
where the cold crisp air cracks across your face
carried on the wind whipping your hair about your
head in a frenzy

While the chill of the evening attacks the
exposed layers of your skin
with spiked fingers raking
causing you to recede into the warmth of your jacket,
you'll find warmth in the subway tunnels
as you hurriedly make your way home

I pray you find an empty
seat where you can rest
heavy legs
and submerge yourself under the waves of the music
coming from your headphones

And as subway doors open
and your tired body instinctually raises itself up,
you'll find the comfort of your bed
and the familiarity of your covers.

You,

I write this letter to you so that on the days
when nostalgia clings to you
like the warmth of freshly done sheets
you'll remember to take a moment to
pause and appreciate the different stages
of your growth

The times of uncertainty the times of unrest
the times where you sat alone
in the library of your mind
where thoughts appear as books sprawled open
revealing pages filled with insecurities, filled with the
times of your deepest pains,
and the times of your greatest joys.

I pray you'll remember them all
and enjoy the comfort of their tender embrace.

I pray you'll hear the voices of the ones
you've touched along the way

I pray you'll see the evidence
of the indelible change in
yourself and each of them

And I pray you'll speak
life over yourself
and those around you.

You,

I write this letter to you
so that you'll remember to be
thankful for where you're at right
now

The places and spaces
      where your spirit finds life, your soul is
refreshed, and your strength is restored.

The places where your comfort is measured
against the rubric of your growth,
      and the spaces where you sit
      like a wallflower
      observing the world
      through your windows

The places where a younger version of
yourself once dreamed it would be on
midsummer nights in the spaces you searched
for adventure

And just like the seasons
change,
you too change
drawing ever closer to the best
version of yourself.

You,

I write this letter to you so that on the days
when rain clouds and gray skies
threaten to offset the pink and orange hues
that flood your bedroom on a sun-kissed afternoon
you'll close the open-ended questions left unanswered
where memories are left empty
        as you search for what it is that sings to your soul

I pray you will let your imagination run
free in the fields of your desires
where your fantasies find flight
and your heart is warmed by comfort fires

For in your universe there is no
limit no space left undefined
no bounds that can contain your spirit
and while pensive thoughts dance with delight
they paint a canvas of pure insight
created out of your curiosity.

You,

I write this letter to you
so that on the days
when you strain against the thoughts
hanging in your mind like dark clouds
feeling like Atlas
with the world on your shoulders
you'll realize that there are times you've been
lost in the beauty of dusk
that paints the sky shades of pink and orange
when the backdrop of the city begins to slowly awake
blinking lights opening

And when familial absences scream
loudly—the silence deafening
you'll catch yourself stealing glances
at the spidery shadows sprawled into the wall
and remember you always have been a
traveler but never walk alone
finding rest in places
shared where spaces
are invaded

and comfort is tested
against the rubric of
growth.

You,

I write this letter to you so that on the days
where you find ambiguity cocooned
in the crawl spaces of your mind,
tempting to erode the foundation of your faith,

and threatening to emerge as full-grown confusion
with chaos in your heart
when you measure yourself against the illusion of the perfect
you:

    The you who gets it right in
          every moment.
              The you who knows what they're
                  doing
                      The you who is a well-crafted version of
                          yourself.

I pray you'll remember that it is not in the mistakes that
fall
        like
ink
        drops
on the pages of your experiences
that define who you are.

Rather,
they add color
to the canvas of the authentic you

And I pray you'll find comfort and peace
as you rest in the presence of the God
who shapes your destiny,
the one who called you from the darkness,
and gave form to
your unshaped essence.

Reflections

17

HOPEFUL & REJUVENATING

You,

I write this letter to you so that on days
where goodbyes become tangible—
felt the moment hugs break tender embrace

Where teary eyes and blurred vision leave
emotions bleeding down your cheeks, you'll
open your heart to it

Embracing heartfelt moments,
small laughs around the
dinner table, late night
strolls rushing to ride
the endless silver mist to
the place you call home.

I pray you'll be reunited
soon with the people who
share the open places in
your chest,
whose lives bring color
to the gray spaces of your life.

You,

I write this letter to you so that on the days
when you find yourself
outside where music
plays in the distance
drowned out by the voices of the crowd
and the spaces in between worlds slowly start to blur

You'll lose and find your sense of
stability as the world starts to feel
off balance and the only anchor
you can find is yourself.

I pray you'll remember
that you're being carved and
chiseled and to enjoy these
moments in time that
always seem so fleeting

And when insecurities try to
claw at you with bony fingers
sharp like daggers—you'll find
your shield well equipped to
handle the barrage.

Reflections

You,

I write this letter to you
so that on the days
when the full moon sits above the
clouds, giving light to the wind kissed
night
where shadows are illuminated
as friends join in laughter,
sharing memories born of love and connection

I pray you remember this feeling of
tenderness as one where your mind is
at ease,
and warm emotions are
given life, stoked by the
flames of intimacy.

You,

I write this letter to you
so that on the days
when the setting sun makes his way
home passing the moon on the way,

You'll cast aside
the burdens of the day
shedding the weight
and leaving worry in your now liberated wake.

And as your footsteps glide
effortlessly across the city floor
as
you traverse the concrete jungle,

I pray you'll find rest and
renewed strength in the hands of
the One who cares for you.

You,

I write this letter to you so that on the days
when you stand on the biggest of stages shoulders squared
chest held high
smile stretched across your lips
with the ones who stood along your way present you'll remember
the journey

Where sleepless nights
bled into exhausted mornings with motivation fleeting energies
draining
and emotions hanging on by threads

I pray you'll remember that success comes in small increments
and each step along the way was preparing you
for what comes next

And I pray you take this moment
to be proud of yourself
and what you achieved
all testaments to your indomitable will.

You,

I write this letter to you so that on the days
where sun-kissed rays hide in overcast skies
as gray clouds hang heavily
carrying with them
the promised rains of sadness,
dropping pit patter on your window
as you lay in the comfort of your blankets
isolated in the darkness of your room mind in the clouds
heart held hostage by prison guards of memories

I pray you'll remember that on the nights
when the moon hides her face, and the night is at his darkest
there is the promise of once hidden rays sprawled brilliantly
casting warm shadows in the morning
giving life to the plants that lounge lazily in your room

I pray you'll remember that
there are diamonds dancing in dew drops
in the garden greens of your soul
where precious memories continuously bloom
granting comfort in the arms of your Creator....

You,

I write this letter to you
so that you'll remember to water your soul
the same way you water the plants
that sit on your windowsill
finding rejuvenation in the rays of the sun

And as you prune yourself
of negative energies and thoughts,
you'll revive your weary spirit
and rekindle the spark of ingenuity that lives inside of you

I pray that you'll find rejuvenation
in the crisp cool air of the morning
that blows through your window
and as the chill runs down your spine

It'll resurrect what once seemed dead
causing your heart to bloom
as old wounds are healed
in the smell of the morning dew.

You,

I write this letter to you so that on the days
when you ride the crowded subway
to and fro' on your day's winding journey

Your eyes scanning the faces that sit across from you
where heads hang listlessly off shoulders
as eyes are held captive by 9:16 scenes

You'll remember that like you they each have their own worries
each have their own fears
each the vices they find corrupting

And as you navigate the outside world where darkness always
seems lurking, I pray you'll remember
that as the light shines within you
you too bear a responsibility to share your light—
one you've always been equipped to bear.

Reflections

You,

I write this letter to you
so that on the days
when shadows sprawl across your
wall echoing the ones in your mind
where tormenting thoughts of ruinous self-doubt
hide like a thief in the night
trying to steal the light of brighter days and
moments where excitement, peace, and joy
meet at the crossroads of passion and purpose

I pray you'll remember to be patient with
yourself as you journey down recovery road, an
unwilling driver in setback's car
fueled by your dreams

I pray that just as your body heals itself through care and
finds itself fortified with your grit and determination,
your mind, spirit and soul will find rest
and rejuvenation
in anticipation of better days to come
where you'll run fleet footed before taking to the sky.

Reflections

You,

I write this letter to you so that on the days
when uncertainty looms like dark clouds
fastly approaching on the horizon,
you will remember that in the most uncertain times,
we find the truth of ourselves:

Where decisions are made
as you find the courage to stand
on the foundations of your faith and character

I pray that you remember
you have the strength to choose the things that you want,
the things that make you content,
and the things that give flight to your dreams.

UPLIFTING & COMFORTING

You,

I write this letter to you so that on the days
when birds cheerily chirp
in the open spaces in which you sit
soaking up the warmth of the sun
like flower petals outstretched
kissed by a gentle breeze

Finally throwing off the load carried all week
where emotions ranged
and feelings ebbed and flowed like the water poured on potted
plants sitting steadfastly on your windowsill

I pray you'll find freedom in the laughter filling the air as you sit in
good company
and I also pray you'll find rejuvenation as you sit alone in the
intimate spaces of your inner thoughts
refreshed by the living waters of life.

Reflections

You,

I write this letter to you so that on the day
when you celebrate the beginning of a new level
the dawn of a new age
and the start of a new chapter

You'll remember the lessons learned
through experiential knowledge
when time, truth, and wisdom
stood as your teachers

Remember to embrace the spaces
where you've learned to exist
in the fullness that you are
where you find freedom to rampantly roam the wilderness
of your untamed thoughts, while curiously tasting the fruits of your
ever evolving desires

I pray that you find delight in the works of your hands,
the endeavors of your mind,
and the idiosyncrasies that underscore the irresistible force you are
as you continue your journey around the sun.

You,

I write this letter to you so that on the days
when motivation flies fleetfooted across forest floors of
distractions,
weighed down by the responsibilities of life
you'll remember to listen to yourself

Listen to the calls from within
as you steady the ship of your mind against negative images and
thoughts from inside
that try to cast you down
and threaten to leave you downtrodden

Never forget that in this
and every moment you are
and always will be enough.

You,

I write this letter to you
So that in the times when doubts circle like vultures
inside of your head,
hanging above the memories you've created
waiting to pick at the flesh of your heart

You will remember who you are in the daylight
where your true self stands tall like buildings reaching the sky
casting shadows where your innermost thoughts hide waiting to be
found

You are stronger than you imagine more resilient than you
comprehend
and when thoughts intended to illuminate feel like they slowly
eliminate
the belief you hold in yourself

Just remember God's got you always.

You,

I write this letter to you so that on the days
where new paths appear
and footsteps steer in unseen directions
as you contemplate the long lists of things
you undoubtedly must do

You'll remember the people in the spaces
who you've laughed with, learned from,
and lived among

You'll remember to take the lessons learned
and one day, when ready,
 use them

Use them to create a life of your own choosing where you are the
most authentic version of yourself—

The one that sits with you alone at 3 am,
the one who often doubts itself
because of the assumptions preconceived notions and limitations
placed by *you*
or those around you

Use them to create
use them to leave the things
and people around you better

I pray you remember that your journey is your own
and only you have the power to shape it
through the decisions you make.

You,

I write this letter to you
so that you'll remember on the dawn of the new month
 to forgive yourself for lessons learned
born from traumas and mistakes of days past

and as you close one chapter
while spring flowers blossom
given new life by torrential downpour

May you find peace and hope
in the memories yet to be created
and experiences to be shared.

You,

I write this letter to you on the days
when depression and anxiety fly first class
through overcast skies of your mind

landing overnights in the innermost sanctuary of your soul
walking through terminal gates of your spirit
as life passes you through tests of your character

Where your comfort is tested against the rubric of your growth as
words are left unspoken
pulled back by the reins of insecurity and guilt

It's on these days I pray you remember
that you are capable of withstanding the treacherous tempest of life
where emotions swirl
blending like colors in your palette as you paint a life

Born of your own creations.

You,

I write this letter to you so that on the days
when the pressures of life
threaten to wrap themselves around you like a python,
constricting every decision,
squeezing until your strength fails,
slowly draining the life of out moments and memories
where fleeting feelings of comfort,
peace, and acceptance blossomed in the garden
greens of your soul.

I pray you'll remember the warmth
of the sun's brilliant rays
as warm kisses planted on your lips,
where serenity reigns supreme,
drowned in the symphony of man and nature blended
as highways cut through parks.

I pray you'll remember to view
yourself like the reflections in the
water, unendingly looking upward
with faith in the promises of better.

Reflections

Reflections

Reflections

Dear Reader,

Our shared journey in "Reflections: A Journey Within" nears its end, but it is merely a pause in the conversation between us. As one book closes, another beckons—a preview of my next endeavor, "Wandering Son." Here, across thirty poems divided into Mind, Soul, and Body, I delve into the themes of spirituality, physicality, and mindfulness.

"Wandering Son" is a testament to the diasporic heartbeat, a song of two worlds—the lush tranquility of Guyanese rainforests and the relentless pulse of American metropolises. It is here, in this liminal space, that my narrative unfurls.

From the sweet remembrances of "Sugar Cane Days" to the sensory tapestry of "Spring In Guyana," and culminating in the rhythmic awakening of "8am in New York," each poem maps the contours of a life lived in-between, of a soul traversing borders, seeking harmony in dissonance.

As we part ways in "Reflections," may you carry forward the assurance that your story, like mine, is one of continuous unfolding, of unyielding growth. Join me soon in the next volume of verse, where every line is a step, every stanza a milestone, on this inexorable march toward self-realization.

With anticipation for our next encounter,
Daniel C. Haynes

Reflections

ABOUT THE AUTHOR

Daniel C. Haynes is a storyteller whose pen is guided by a profound connection to his Guyanese roots, imbuing his work with richness and warmth. As a journalist, he turns words into windows to view the soul of society, capturing the unspoken tales that lie at the heart of the human condition. In the realm of education, he stands as a mentor who inspires through the power of relatable storytelling. Daniel's commitment to his craft is not just about sharing stories—it's about fostering a deeper understanding and appreciation for the narratives that unite us.

www.ingramcontent.com/pod-product-compliance
Lightning Source LLC
LaVergne TN
LVHW051607080426
835510LV00020B/3183